Lead the Way

By

Persuasion

- The simplest way of influencing-

Laura Ion

CONTENTS

ACKNOWLEDGMENTS

From Laura

I decided to write this book, after having the most inspiring conversation about how to practice non verbal and verbal persuasion, how to be persuasive and sell everything from beliefs, values, feelings to products, using our verbal and nonverbal communication, body language and eye contact.

This book has attitude, this book is a She or a He, you, the reader, you choose! What stays for sure, is that the book speaks from the "I".

I would like to thank Chip Gautreaux for being by my side while writing this book, for his assistance, keen eye and on target feedback.

Many thanks go also to Dr. Richard Bandler and John La Valle who inspired, influenced and amazed me.

Lead The Way by Persuasion

Chapter 1

HOW OLD IS PERSUASION?

After the amazing journey I had in Orlando, I returned home with plenty of questions in my mind, a lot of feelings and doubts….my beliefs were so tried and me, I was flying on clouds of new ways and new beginnings. None of the seminars were meant to answer to my questions and as Thomas D'Aquino said: *"When God loves somebody, he intrigues him, gives him no peace but endless desire to discover His immense Creation- Human Being"*

I had no peace, but doubts, although my reason for flying to America was to find the peace!

While flying back to Romania, I was questioning myself, answering to those questions but feeling still dissatisfied, wondering if the theories I had, could manage in practice.

Persuasion Engineering seemed to me rather like a Harvard subject and I do not refer here to the content of the seminar, but to the name itself that sounded in my head like the music of Bach to a lunatic:" Peeeeersuasionnnnn Engineeeeeering!

Suddenly, Dr. Bandler woke me up with his impetuous voice and his tremendous inflections: *"People, should always pay attention to the names!"* and I was paying attention to the names.

My brain was paying attention to questions. What was in fact persuasion? How old is it? Is it verbal only? If I had no tongue, and vocal cords could I persuade? What about eyes and posture? Could I persuade more with eyes and with my body then with my words?

Then, I started to think of the age of persuasion, so, I went back to Adam and Eve, the right beginning for everything. I was wondering If Eve persuaded Adam to take the apple or just manipulated him. But what is the difference between persuasion and manipulation? The only answer that came in to my mind was: benefits, win-win rapport. So, if Eve had promised Adam to have sex after taking the apple…then we can talk about persuasion. I was not thinking about money at that time, sex being the only "good" used as trade. If Eve just commanded to Adam to bring the apple without giving him something in return, we can talk about manipulating. I don't even care if she was nice or not, she used her body to fool him, as long he got nothing, we just talk about manipulation. Who could help me with all these questions? I might go to theology or maybe read the Bible again, but as far as I remember, Adam and Eve never spoke to each other. I consider this a fair dilemma and I will leave it on the edge of human frustration similar to "Who was the first: the hen or the egg?"

My question still stays: How old is persuasion?

I was listening again to Dr. Bandler and being focused on finding the answer to my question, I was tracing his words like a worm, eager to find the perfect hole underground. I was so energized and ready to put down on my notebook the answer, that my head was betting like being in a Las Vegas casino. Then I stopped. I stopped even my breathing as if I was underwater, and then I asked myself: "What if God decided to give us the persuasion ability, influencing capacity when he decided to make us different: woman and man, female and male?" What's the point to persuade somebody who is almost like you, who has almost similar needs, who can never surprise you, more than you can surprise yourself, who can never give you something that you can't get, especially when you live in God's Eden and you have everything?

Let's go back to Adam and Eve, and let's see why persuasion was good for them? They were alone, nothing to sell and nothing to buy, as they had everything for free in Eden, everything except sex. Procreation was like God's will and in change for sex, Adam must give Eve food and security for example. Probably the economists will say that we are talking about one buyer- Adam and one seller- Eve, and being no competition there is no need for persuasion and everything was about seduction.

But seducing is persuading, influencing. I would say that as long as both had the possibility to choose- one to offer the pleasure, the other one to offer the security and food, we can talk about persuasion. You see, *persuasion* comes when you have the possibility to *choose*, when you have other options, inactivity is an option too.

I do believe that persuasion is one of the most famous gifts that we got since our beginnings in this fascinating world of continuing negotiation. What's the meaning of Persuasion if Diversity would never exist? Because, you see, where the *equality* lays both in chances and resources, there is no use for *persuasion, for influence.* I can conclude that persuasion is an immense tool that makes the difference.

Making the difference, this is the point!

 I was flying over the Atlantic Ocean and I was thinking in a loud voice, "Who persuaded me to fly over the Atlantic Ocean, when I was so afraid of the idea of flying over the oceans and seas?" I persuaded myself and where this persuasion lays on? How did I know that I have to persuade myself so hard so as to have the courage to fly? Was I making any kind of terminology confusion between Self Motivation and Self Persuasion? I started to question and search in my 'brain dictionary' for an answer, I asked my heart and my body to feel that answer. You know, there is no use for searching and finding an answer in your brain if you don't feed your heart and body with it and create *feelings*.

All the while, I was flying along and I was staring at the ocean and questions hit my mind like at a bowling game. When I said Self Motivation, like reading a page in a dictionary, I felt something strong hit me straight in my heart and in my brain. There was a huge cocktail of love and passion, feeling like being on the peak of an iceberg, nothing was stronger than this…but where was Self Persuasion?

I was looking more for Self Persuasion, as long as Self Motivation subject was very clear to me.

Motivation was the trigger, because, Dr. Bandler and his seminars are memorable, and I was going there, having been hypnotized by his magic way of being himself, so authentic. But still, what was in it for me? I gained self awareness, new and amazing piece of information, new abilities, new ways of doing things, new people….and God, there is an endless list of tremendous benefits! For all these things I didn't feel like I had a *strategy* to sell to myself the seminars. So, I was self motivated to do this.

Self Motivation needs no steps, no strategy because the native passion, looking like that passion you genetically inherited, requires no selling process. Where that kind of passion and love live, motivation is at its home! Passion and love can sell anything, they are genuine, they both are home for motivation and this is why when you do things from and with passion, you are convincible by default, self motivation being stronger than self persuasion.

Self Motivation is like a blind, yet strong person with a big heart; and she is so strong as to need no strategy to convince about moving forward, going and getting something. What else makes self motivation being so strong, I have no idea, but I know that she can make you move the mountains, do the craziest things in the world, win all the battles with fears and worries you have. Self Motivation is a "she" for sure!

Self Persuasion, instead, is like a weak person, smart, with big open eyes always having a strategy in order to move yourself forward, to make you wish so damn hard something that nothing can stop you. *So, every time when you go and get something done, accomplished and feel like you had a strategy behind,* you have specific answers to:

- What's in it for me?
- What do I have to do for that in return?

you do know that what moved you to action was Self Persuasion.

Isn't it strange the way we are meant to be? We have the possibility to choose when to sell to ourselves and when to go and get something just because we feel that way, and we feel that so strong, that we need no explanations for our reasons and no particular purpose for gaining.

Chapter 2

WHERE DOES PERSUASION LIVE?

I was walking on my mind like on the enlightened streets of New York City, and as I was flying over it, I felt like being a homeless stranger in my own brain. God, this was amazing!

As I knew that iceberg metaphor of Freud, I started trembling with fear, and wonders, and God knows how many other feelings! I was so deeply afraid what I might have inside my brain and having the flashlight in my hand, I decided to look for persuasion.

"Can I get you something?" the stewardess got me grounded and present with her beautiful warm smile.

"I am looking for a particular sort of thing….but

water would be fine!"

While she was pouring water, I was watching the way the water was transferred from bottle to glass and I exclaimed: "That's it!!"

Persuasion is like a big bottle of water and we can get how much water we want, any time we feel we need to. But persuasion must be more than a bottle….and I feel it is not like liquid, it is more like grains of sand, or pieces of a puzzle, why not say?

So, after deciding the shape, being so important, I was wondering how these sand grains are stored in our mind. How do we know what ingredients to put in order to influence people around us? How much sand grains? What kind of sand grains? Where is this sand stored exactly?

Now, the easiest way to establish a hierarchy or a rule or a behavior pattern is to go from particular to general, to pick up the best examples ever and explore them.

Here was my question: How could Nelson Mandela or Martin Luther King be so inspiring and persuasive without raising any questions regarding their educational background, diplomas and so on?

I was talking to many people that heard Mandela speaking, I've been listening to Martin Luther King's speech for many times and he inspired me, convinced me, and not even a second I was thinking about if he is entitled or not to influence people, to talk about freedom, equality and peace. And you know what, you don't have to have a bachelor degree or a PHD to talk about values, beliefs and principles.

To influence genuinely you need to go deep down to your roots where your nature laid your values, listen to their voice and live them every day of your life.

All of a sudden, my brain visualized a pyramid, and I called it the Pyramid of Persuasion. Here is the design of the Pyramid, the description of its structure and process!

The Pyramid of Persuasion

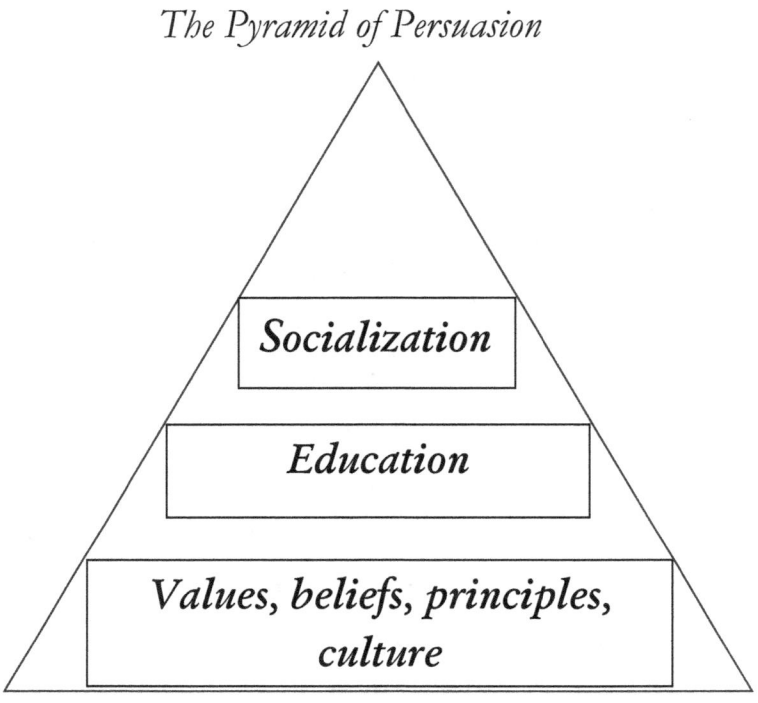

At the base of the pyramid stays what I call the amazing world of values, beliefs, principles and culture-they define us and make us become unique, match with other people around us, creating network and communicating.

Values, beliefs and principles are at the base of the pyramid, meaning that if we persuade from here, we'll be genuine, credible and powerful, 100% of persuasion process coming from here, has 100% chances to success. Your own values say "who you are", "where do you want to go", "how do you work".

Think about this! Let's say you are a sales person, selling cars. One day there comes a family having kids with them and they want to buy a family car. You have to persuade them to buy one of the most expensive and safety cars. It is said that one of the most common values that bring people together is the value of love represented by family. If you come and persuade this family from your value of love, you have 100% chance to be genuine, authentic, inspiring, and your eyes will glitter like the purest lakes of Alaska.

Think about matching your value of love with their value of love! Could they resist to you, with your way of being magic and authentic like having *the best interest* ever?

You see, in sales, the big question ever asked by clients is if the sales person wants to sell services or products only from target/money perspective or if there is indeed a genuine interest in what's good and proper for their needs. If you come to persuade from the base of pyramid you will blow this question away like pulling the curtain of doubts and fears that covers the client's eyes. You could also bring with you personal examples that sustain in practice your value, in this case value of love. Talk about how important was for your mother to bring your kids to school in a very safe car. You will talk about your kids, your mother, your family, and you will match them, creating the connection as the bridge between goals and accomplishments. I have been working in sales more than 10 years as a sales person and as people manager, coordinating sales teams. One of the most stupid things I ever heard was to practice the following as you practice bungee jumping:

- eye contact
- being present and grounded
- voice projection

No way! Nobody succeeded in this, and do you know why? Because these three major things are just the *effect* of that power that lives inside us: *values and beliefs.*

We should practice living the values first, and then we'll have no problem in having eye contact, in being present and grounded or having one of the most inspiring voices ever. Let's work with our nature, make us live our way without learning scripts, as bad actors, having the same show every time and no one listening to what they say.

The second level of pyramid talks about *education*. I call this level, the level where you can specialize and differentiate your persuasion process, being competitive and grounded due to the information you use in order to treat objections.

Persuasion must come from the base (values, beliefs and culture) and then take some more power from the second level.

Now, let's take the same example with the sales person, selling cars. If that person has a diploma in cars engineering and he has knowledge about cars, technologically speaking, he can build two major things in his relationship with the customer:

- *Trust-* coming from values and beliefs. You gain people' trust when you are genuine, when you talk from your values to their values, from your beliefs to their beliefs and you enrich all of these with knowledge
- *Appreciation-* coming from the value added to the persuasion process, due to education background.

Appreciation comes from inoculating and treating people' objections and you can do this while talking from education level, using specific piece of specialized information.

It is something huge that you can achieve while persuading, and that is the cocktail of *trust and appreciation*.

It is like you pour into a glass some red wine, a drop from the ocean and fresh mint. Strange combination but deadly drink to the people listening to you, because:

- Everyone's desire is to feel the ocean and its immensity like knowledge;

- Everyone would try at least once in a lifetime to get drunk from the most genuine and perfect wine having deep roots as values and beliefs;

- Fresh mint reminds everyone to come back and take more cocktail next time and make the most out of the experience.

"Making the most of it!" it is one of my favorite imperative phrases, because it is so inspiring and so moving that I need nothing but myself in order to have success. Making the most of it is one of my friend's favorite slogans too. He is a doctor, a very good one, but when it comes about connecting to people he is like a very beautiful frigid woman. He is petrified and he talks only from medicine perspective using only medical terms and you all know that this could be very disturbing, confusing and worrying for all of us who have no medical background. This man came to one of our coaching sessions, telling me that he wishes his clients know how good he is as a doctor, that he really cares about their condition and he really deserves their fully appreciation and confidence.

While coaching, he realized that he had a very bad plan for his patients: he was persuading them to follow the treatment, to trust him as a doctor, talking to them from the second level of the pyramid: education. He never went down at the base of the pyramid: values and beliefs. That's why, when he talked to his patients, he was so much into being a doctor, that he forgot how to be a human being. In the end, he decided to apply this persuasion pyramid tool. Two days later, around ten o'clock he called me with excitement in his voice and he said:

"God, it works!"

I asked him:

"Are you surprised?"

Why was he surprised to live his own values and be walk the talk? He had these values but never acknowledged them, blaming the time for not letting him do this. Now, he told me that he went to his patients always having in his mind his father who won the battle with a cruel disease. He was by his father's side, first as a human being and them as a doctor. His value of love was represented by his father, and he knew that the value of love brings uniqueness, especially to a doctor. This is how he made the difference! Now, he was living his value buy keeping his father's experience alive in his brain and heart. I asked him to feel this experience and remember it every time he meets patients. Living his values, this is how he became genuine and authentic! Then, he noticed people' reactions when he came to persuade them, talk about their condition and what are the next steps to be taken, as he was practicing persuasion as the pyramid model says: when going for persuasion or influence, always start with your own *values*, then, enrich the process using your *education*al background and finally, bring in your *social* skills.

He told me he no longer felt that barrier between he and his patients, their eyes were meeting his eyes, and he could have eye contact, be present and grounded and the inflections of his voice produced mimics on their faces.

This is what I call a mixture between empathy and persuasion and there are so many jobs and situations that require empathy and persuasion, that you should practice persuasion pyramid daily, even during the night in your dreams.

This friend of mine gained trust, respect and appreciation.

He gained self peace, self acknowledgement and now, if you wake him any time during the night, he can tell by his heart what his values and beliefs are, the way he is living them.

The third level of the pyramid is represented by *socialization* and this is mostly about that ability of working with others, communicating and creating networks. Being on the top, socialization is like the chocolate you put on a vanilla ice cream, it makes the difference to that flavor. But still, a vanilla ice cream without chocolate, would be just a simple vanilla ice cream.

So, if we take the same example we had, with that sales person selling cars, and we decided that he persuaded from the base of pyramid, then he fed the process with education, now it is time to add the flavor that makes the difference- *Socialization.*

Imagine this! An inspiring guy that gives you that feeling of calm and security, that says a hello looking into your eyes, is paying attention to everything you say, is clarifying all the issues before jumping to conclusions…that guy is a fantastic communicator when comes to you! He matches you, and seeing your family, he brings his value of love with him, makes that value be alive in that moment. His eyes are bigger and he is eating your words, making you feel like he is being there just for you. He talks about security, and guess what, safety and family security is everything to you, and that guy, a stranger sales person, matches you, having the same values as you have. You know what, this is like synchronic swimming, your values are dancing together and this is how he comes to blow away any of your fears and objections.

Fears and objections can ruin everything! And here we are, having the most simple and pleasant tool to apply: the pyramid of persuasion. The magic rule is to go from down to top and to feel each of these three levels, because it is about you. And when it is about you, you give the best of you to make the most of it. Making the most of it could mean everything to people around you, but what stays for sure, is that it will always be about treating fears and objections.

Some of the fears we have, we were born with. Depending on our particularities and situations, we just amplify them, minimize them or create new ones. This pyramid is like a management tool kit for fears. Think about the marvelous things that people can do *after getting the treatment against fears* from:

- someone who is speaking from his/her *Values and Beliefs*, and that someone is living his/her values;

- someone that is answering to the questions and he/she is treating the objections using his/her *Educational background*;

- someone that knows the best way to match you and has the best *Social* skills!

You will trust that kind of person and *trust means lack of fear.* This is the cure I see for fears and objections: *Trust, like trusting yourself and people around you.*

The magic of this pyramid consists in going, as I said before, from down to top and never from top to down or miss one of the three levels. It is like building a house: you never start with the roof, you start with the foundation and the stronger the foundation it is, the stronger the house becomes and it stands still in front of any hurricanes or other disasters. You can never have a *real house* if you build that house without a roof or the rooms necessary to survive or to make the difference between a common house and a competitive house that can get the highest price on the market.

While flying from New York to Paris, I was the 'lucky' person of a turbulent flight. And, as if nothing could go worse than this, I had to take care of someone's fears and persuade her using, unconsciously, this pyramid of persuasion. God, I even didn't mean to do this, like having a strategy before, so as to use this pyramid very clear and specific! Everything was so natural, and I thought we might have this pyramid like a huge dragon that is sleeping inside us, without knowing it or acknowledging the levels. This is how I found out that, under panic or extreme situations, our brain knows very well where to search for the best persuasion process. The key is to trust your mind, your naked mind, and not to come and give directions, because when being directive you have the chances to ruin what nature built perfectly.

I took this lady's hand and looked into her eyes, copying her head movement and eyes movement and I brought in the reflective process- copying her words too.

"This is it, my girl! This is going to be the end of my story!"

"No, ma'am, this is not going to be the end of your story, or my story! I don't have such a plan! Do you? "

She smiled and she laid down on her chair like being ready to go on trance. When smiling, I knew she had a chance.

"You know, my mother was afraid of flying too and she started to have heart problems, because every time she had a flight, she panicked and she was living like on the top of a cliff, every second ready to fall down. This was a bad plan she chose to have. She decided to take care of her heart and have pleasant and relaxing flights, and this was a good plan! "

"See, if my mother could do this I have no doubts that you are able to do this. She was worse than you and she succeeded in! "

"And, by the way, Air France is a very good airline company. I enjoy flying with them and I trust the pilots and the stewards too."

"Pay attention to the pilot's voice! Can you feel the confidence he is spreading around? "

"I am a psychologist and I can read people….and there is nothing he is hiding from us, trust me! "

All the way I was talking to her. I kept her hand and looked in to her eyes. She was calm and ready to watch…a movie.

"Here we are, my dear! I think Casablanca is a good choice, and when we land in Paris all you'll have in your mind will be just "Play it again, Sam!"

She was so relaxed, and no worries I could see on her face. This was amazing! I was talking to her from my values of love represented by my family, then I used my knowledge to sustain what I said about the Air France pilot, and all the time I used my "working with others" abilities to persuade her.
This was the magic of the Pyramid of Persuasion!

Chapter 3

THE BEST TRADE EVER

I have joined lots of seminars and workshops, so far, both as a student and as a trainer. I remember that, when people spoke about *sex, money and food*, everyone's attention was attracted to these three topics as if the strongest punch ever, woke them up. As a trainer you never get the chance to miss someone and if you are going to use all of these three things in a one context, or during the same seminar, you have 100% chances to match everybody in the room. Yes, I can say I used this trick many times when I saw that people were about to "leave" me with myself just because they were tired or hungry , or…and it worked!

These three topics that represent one of the most common values among people around the world (the value of security might be represented by money, the value of love could be represented by sex in some cases and the value of safety could be represented by food, for some people) intrigued me a lot. I felt them like tools for persuading, influencing or even seducing, according to the circumstances occurred. I can say, I was charmed by the power of sex and sexuality more as a definition for women, than as a definition of a physical or biological act. In my opinion, sex and sexuality at their best, should be used in order to seduce and seducing is a way of persuading, of influencing. While I was thinking about this, lots of examples that really changed the history of our world crossed my mind.

Just think about the most well known examples in the history, like King Henry III, King of France, when he gave his ships to Venice after having a liaison with Veronica Franco, who was one of the best courtesans that Venice ever had. And Venice is the best example of politics and diplomacy: using beauty, intelligence and talent creating the most gifted women, the courtesans, to ensure national freedom, peace and friendship. This was a very good example of a national persuasion process!

Now, I would like you to invite on a trip now-a-days, and think about being as persuasive as Veronica Franco was, and sell cars or houses whatsoever, as she sold her intelligence combined with beauty in a privileged sexual act for a prosperous life. Venice had the best strategy ever, in my opinion, because history proved that women can change everything, therefore Venice decided that the most beautiful, intelligent, well educated, well mannered women should become courtesans- and this was a privilege. Let's have a close look upon this woman, Veronica Franco.

She was beautiful and she had strong values being inspired by her mother. One of her values was the value of love, and she described that value in her poems too. Her value of love was represented by the opposite sex and during that time nothing evil or immoral was under this kind of value. Coming to persuade her lovers, powerful people from the government of Venice, only from her value of love combined with her beauty, it was not enough. She had to study a lot: literature, geography, history, mathematics, manners, music and so many other things, and therefore she became more persuasive, and sustained her value of love and beauty with education. She became more powerful and she convinced men that she was the best choice no matter the situation was. She gained a fortune, name and place in the history of that time, because she persuaded people around her that any price is worth it when it comes about her. Values and education were not enough, and something else was supposed to make the difference- socializing, as the ability of creating network and working great with others. She was a poet and communication proved to be a strong point of Veronica, but, in order to succeed in having the best social skills, she needed practice and she practiced. Due to her talent, hard work and enriched social skills, she became the only woman having poems in an Anthology of poems at that time. To be in that anthology and remain in the history, she had to do more than seducing powerful men of Venice, she had to persuade them.

Nobody thought about Veronica Franco like dealing with a specific well designed persuasion process because she didn't…it was in her nature. She acknowledged and lived her values, she trusted and accessed education but mainly, she soft skilled her social abilities, made them sharper. This is how she became inspiring, able to move people around her, influence them.

I couldn't ignore beauty, because beauty attracted men, but you see, beauty itself is nothing, it might work one time, but this is going be all about. People, and I mean smart people need more to be persuaded to give something in return. Even their coming back again and again to the same beautiful woman is the result of the persuasion not of beauty only. History always taught us great lessons to be remembered, and the history of the courtesans and mainly the history of Veronica Franco, taught us that persuasion is a matter of living, living our own values, and then is a matter of learning, learning from others and from our own mistakes, and finally it is a matter of connecting, connecting with our inner world and connecting with others.

Never do the mistake of reducing the name of a courtesan just to sexuality and depravation, because this could be one of the biggest mistakes! Never see this example only as a matter of beauty and seduction! A beautiful painting is nothing if the colors say no story, create no feelings and no memories. Take this is as an example, and every time you want to go and persuade yourself and your children, your friends or your clients, think you are a Veronica Franco, that Veronica able to live genuinely her values, who never gives up on education and who knows how to work with others at the highest standards.

Acknowledge and live your values, bring your values with you in your mind's pocket and heart 's vessels, learn, change and adapt, work with other people as if they are part of your present and future and make the most of the moments you spend with them. All above, bring your beauty because God created beauty in so many different ways and He gave us beauty under so many faces that we should be smart enough and we should know how to bring this to the surface as beauty is the cover of the most precious book about our depths and heights, seen and unseen, conscious and unconscious.

Practice persuasion this way and I can assure you that there is nothing able to stop you from being genuine, authentic, smart and reliable and you'll make the most of it all the time, getting success and success is about everything.

I love flying with big planes on long distances and this is because I have time enough for meditation, for self questioning, for reading, watching movies or creating network. This time chose to watch movies, and I took 'Cleopatra: Queen of Egypt'.

I read quite a lot about Egypt and the Ptolemaic dynasty and this movie was a great chance to practice my imagination, to live with Cleopatra during that time. Practicing my imagination was in fact a simple way of testing my theory about the pyramid. Was Cleopatra's success upon those two famous men, Marc Anthony and Caesar, a matter of persuasion or manipulation? If we want to do this dissection, let's find out more about Cleopatra!

The last Ptolemaic queen of Egypt, Cleopatra made herself attractive with "charm and sweetness in the tones of her voice". Cassius Dio said:"she possessed a most charming voice and knowledge and the knowledge of how to make herself agreeable to everyone. She was brilliant to look upon and to listen to". I would love to pay attention to what Cassius Dio said and I refer here to knowledge that belongs to the *education* level in the pyramid, and knowledge of how to make herself agreeable, this being the *socialization* level in the pyramid, agreeable while connecting with other people around her. As far as I know, Cassius Dio, never spoke about her values, and this is because, her main value was so obvious that needed no presentation. Cleopatra was in love with Egypt throne and therefore in love with the power of ruling and everything she did came from her way of acknowledging and living this value. Cleopatra was practicing my pyramid and I don't think she ever imagined that she went through a process while persuading, having a specific leveled strategy, in order to have some influence over Caesar and Marc Anthony. She was for sure a great strategist and a master in art of persuasion. Just think about the fact that she gained Caesar's military support and assured Egypt peace and prosperity. In change of this, Caesar assured that Egypt provides its riches to Rome Empire. As far as history speaks there was a win-win situation: Cleopatra ruled Egypt and she kept the throne she was in love with, while Caesar took advantages from using Egypt as an immense source of grain and military techniques.

In his masterpiece, "Life of Anthony", Plutarch said that:"judging by the effect of her beauty and knowledge upon Caius Caesar, she had hopes that she would more easily bring Anthony to her feet" and she did. She proved to be versatile and able to adapt as wind that had blown in Rome Empire. When she felt that Caesar's power and influence was questioned by the Senate, and Marc Anthony became stronger and stronger, she decided to persuade him. Some of us might say that it was only a matter of love, she had fallen in love with Marc Anthony, but I say still it was a matter of persuasion. The love for the throne of Egypt was above her love for men, and she was that brilliant to persuade herself that any price was worth it, therefore she could persuade any of men around her, that she was one of a kind. Her goal from the very beginning was to have by her side fully committed powerful men, both Caesar and Marc Anthony and doing this she solidified her grip on the throne. I think there is no woman that wouldn't love to be a Cleopatra, one way or another, and I was smiling while watching the movie, having this in my mind. Some of us could question these two examples, and it is their right to do this. They could bring under prospection the moral and virtues points of view for both Veronica and Cleopatra, or the subject developed latter in the history by Immanuel Kant: "*Never use people as way of getting things done, obtaining goals, but always as main purposes*" and I would like to salute their sense of adventure, hunger for information and thirst for revealing the unrevealed.

This book wants to talk more about the Pyramid of Persuasion, the way this pyramid works in real life situations, about its success. I promise you to talk later on about moral and virtues, about using or not using people, about who was the first: the hen or the egg?

When it comes about persuasion process, women have a great advantage born with, and this is beauty and sexuality. Now, I am convinced that neither Veronica nor Cleopatra could go so far and gain so much without beauty and sexuality. But beauty and sexuality are not enough and even if seducing is a way of persuading, you have to come up with much more. Is there any woman that says she never used her beauty and her sexuality to persuade more, to get things done quicker, sooner, better? I am using this daily and it is giving me confidence, power, making me shine and be more brilliant, because I am positive that, our mind is one and the same with our body as a sailor is one and the same with his boat. It is nothing immoral or impolite to use your beauty and sexuality in order to persuade, it is just about knowing the limits and respecting people we interact with, having win-win situation and fair affairs.

As I said in the beginning of this chapter, I was charmed by the power of sex and sexuality more as a definition for women, than as a definition of a physical or biological act Indeed, beauty and sexuality sell a lot, and make people to be open, calm and relaxed, sometimes distracted, and this is why when closing deals for billions, business men take beautiful and smart women with them. See, persuasion begins with beauty but never ends due to beauty, thinking and matching are the core of any deal.

What could be more successful than a beautiful, smart and well mannered person that is able to learn, change and adapt? Learning, changing and adapting sounds like a self-education process, but it is much more than this. Self-education, the way it works now-a-days, it is more about learning and sometimes about changing, as an effect of the learning process, it is not about *adapting*. The best trade you can ever do with yourself is to sell what you learnt, then sell what you became, and sell your personal way of adapting to other people and to the world itself.

I have been talking to many people during recruiting process I have done for about 6 years, and I have never seen someone really able and eager to sell himself/herself. They were so much afraid of selling their knowledge, what they have learned, afraid of selling their new abilities, those developed or those enriched/changed after learning process. They seemed to be ashamed of their own educational background and professional skills and they looked like people scared of not being discovered. To me it was so strange, that I decided to have a closer look upon some of those people. What they had in common was lack of trust, fear of unknown, love for routine and low expectations.

First of all, it was a matter of trust, they didn't trust themselves as if someone, a sort of "bad guy" that lived inside them, could uncover them when a certain stimuli occurred. This is why they loved routine, they had time to predict the stimuli occurrence. Let me explain to you what really happened to them, by describing a concept I gave born: *the Spiral of Existence.*

The Spiral of Existence

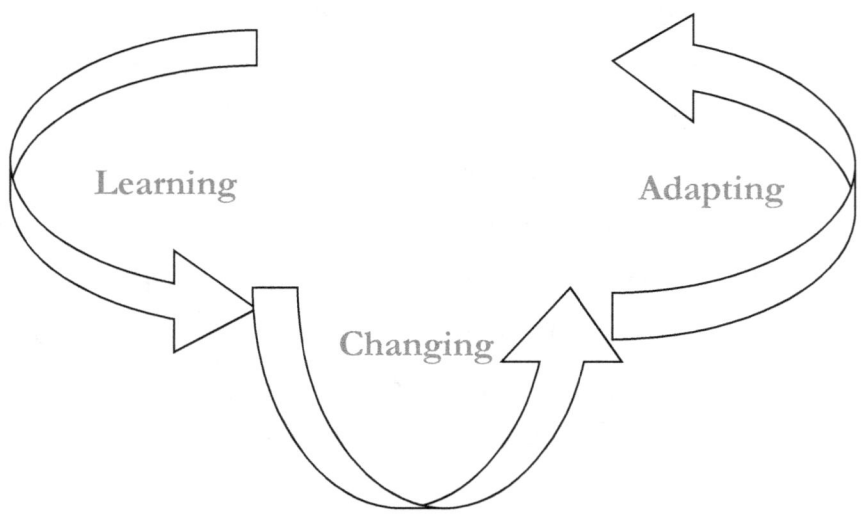

This *Spiral of Existence* speaks about the way these three major stages: *Learning, Changing and Adapting* live together, interact and influence our behavior and our entire existence.

Imagine that this amazing gift that we call life it is about:

- Learning – it is the process of assimilating information and we start learning things from the very first day of our lives. Even since we are babies, we learn how to keep our parents as much as we want close to us and this is by crying when they leave our room. We learn our first steps, first words, feelings and till the last day of our lives, we strive for learning sometimes consciously, sometimes involuntarily but always we keep learning.

- Changing is a consequence of the learning process, showing that the information we accessed was able to modify something inside us. It is a way of measuring the success of the learning process. If change never comes, the information we get is just a piece of information.

In an ideal world, any piece of information should produce changes, because learning and changing together go to development, and development is the measure of God's success in creating his piece of art: Human Being.

I may say therefore that it is mandatory that the learning process to produce changes, but is this what really happens in reality? Do we measure every time the success of the learning process? If the answer is yes, how do we do this? Some of us might say that the evaluation process is a way of validating the changes that learning process produced. The evaluation process validates only the rate of assimilating the information, the theories, the concepts. To validate and measure the changes, you need time and a specific process that shows *what* piece of information, discipline or theory produced *what* change, and then what are the *benefits* that the changing process brought to that person.

Are we really ready to measure the changing process and its consequences? I mean ready to be smart and specific, to see what disciplines produce more changes and what disciplines produce quicker changes for example? What piece of information has the greatest impact on people as rate and as degrees of impact? Think about having answers to these questions, to know what really happens, to have an acknowledged changing process! Do you see how close success could be to us?

It would be like knowing exactly what drawer has

the key that unlocks the changing process as a tool to become smarter, happier and more successful. Nothing stays still in this world, and in order to survive, we have to be much more open to change, we have to acknowledge and pay attention to it, we have to recognize that while going throw a changing process, we take a step closer to success and plenitude. Pay attention to everything you do and wonder every time you read something, you learn something or you debate something:

"What is this going to change inside me?"

"How do I know this?"

"What are the effects of these changes upon me and upon people around me?"

Sometimes it is better not to find the answer in a book you read, because there are so many chances that the answer to be wrong for you, or brings to life bad memories (It has happened to me many times) that you will forget the book. The mystery of a good book is to be read again and again, like a beautiful and mysterious woman loved by her man. So I prefer to ask questions, make you wonder and search, because you know, asking questions make you smarter, make you discover new maps and new territories. A good book never gives you wings to fly, unless you understand that reading it, you owe it two things: *to learn how to change and how to adapt.*

- Adapting is about everything, it is the end of the changing process and the beginning of a new learning processes.

It is not enough to make changes and to acknowledge them, you have to do more in order to be successful, and this is to adapt. You see, there are so many quotes about change as a process and as a tool too, so many books about tools that help you make changes and support you during changing process, but only a few speak about the adapting process.

Have you ever questioned why so many people are so successful while changing, they go perfectly for a while and then they go back to their former habits? It happens in every field, starting with to middle and top management people, leaders to those people involved in therapies for drugs, drinking, gambling or food addiction. Is there anyone monitoring and supporting them in order to be successful going through adapting process? How do they do this? If they go back to their former habits it is not a consequence of changing failure, but a consequence of non existing specific adapting process.

They might change their behavior and habits for a while, but this doesn't mean that the old behavior is annihilated or the bad habit is somewhere in a box, thrown away in their brain. If the new path created in the brain is not strong enough and matched to the reality, it is just a matter of time for the old path to take the new path's place. This is why, during adapting process, people should convince themselves that, the new path created is on its feet, strong enough to face reality and people around, stay grounded no matter how high the waves are or how strong the wind blows while the former stimuli is meeting their brain.

Here is the question that makes the difference: "How do you know that the new path is strong enough?" meaning that you really completed the adapting process and the former stimuli brings no memory back and no bad behavior as it happened in the past. In order to validate the adapting process you have to do a sort of a check list by:

- Asking feedback
- Noticing people reactions as a response to your new behavior (usually the responses are preceded by emotions. Mimics give all the clues. So, pay attention to mimics of the people you meet! Pay attention to their non verbal communication!)
- Meeting again the former stimuli that caused you the bad response and therefore you created a bad behavior. If the former stimuli brings back no bad behavior, not even like a memory, then you adapted to the environment and the new path works.

Imagine someone that was food addicted and he/she learned how to eat healthy. Now, you give him/her the chance to be the chef, and bad behavior never comes back although food is everywhere. What we can say is that, the spiral of existence was closed and the adapting process was completed. Now, that person is not only able to live and practice the adapting process, but to create new requirements and opportunities for learning. Therefore he/she might learn how to be a *gourmet* although in the past he/she was a *gourmand.* This is progress and development, and the spiral never ends. People that are able to complete the stages of their spiral are successful people. You can recognize them easily because they are present and grounded, they have eye contact, they are confident and their voice will always say to buy them. They are the greatest deal someone could ever make, and they do the best trade ever with themselves.

Can you imagine how easy it is like to persuade anyone to buy anything you sell when you are genuine, able to learn, change and adapt? People buy happiness, confidence and success, and this is what the completed spiral of existence brings.

Chapter 4

HOW DO YOU KNOW?

Do you really know how it feels like to look for a lifetime that question that makes the difference, gives you an answer, that answer that makes you cry in the loudest voice ever heard: "That's it!!!"?

How many times do we take decisions and then we question ourselves if they were right, or if we could have done better? I can tell you that I did this hundreds of times, and I had many nights going to bed still questioning, and waking up in the morning with no answer.

All I have seen was just a pair of blue smart eyes, capturing the entire room and hundreds of eyes. All I have heard was just a strong and peaceful voice whose projection smashed my brain ready to go in a trance…of course unconsciously.

Dr. Bandler gave me the answer to my questions by providing the simplest question I ever heard: " How do you know? "

Day one of the seminar was like I landed in the country of "How do you know?" That was the question of the day, it ruled my night and the next morning too as if it was a sort of addiction. That's it! I was addicted to this question and I started to inquire my entire life as if my brain was in a trial court waiting for the sentence of his life: good or wrong!

We are always looking for complex questions and answers, as if complexity is always a smart and an academic thing. Simplicity was given to humanity as a divine gift, because God himself is simple, and the things He created are simple, connected and part of an immense chain called life chain.

Just think about the animals that have fur or skin similar to the environment they live, I refer here to their color and shape. Don't you think it was the simplest way in which God could give them the chance to have a smart fight for their lives when the situation occurred? Wouldn't have been to complex, difficult and even useless to give for example sharp long teeth to a quite small iguana instead of skin changing capacity? Therefore an iguana is able to adapt to the environment it belongs to, and to hide easily from the predators. This is why matching is smarter than any weapon and the simple way is always the smartest way.

Or, let's have a look on our children! Do you see how smart and simple they are? Their questions are the most difficult questions to us, just because we decided to look for complex answers, and we decided to have the bad plan of choosing the curvy way instead of the straightway.

"Why?" question is the question of a 3-4 years old child. Around this age, children keep asking "Why?" and we keep staring at them, as if they are disabled aliens, unable to see and understand. This question precedes "how do you know?" question and if the first one goes to *reason,* the second one goes to *feelings* and both live in the *brain.* It is right and natural to go first to reason and then to feelings.

In my opinion, when children ask you questions starting with a "Why?" and then continue with a "How do you know?" is because the brain is structured to go first: to the reason or to the root of the cause and then to add the feeling to that reason or cause. In my opinion, this is not a random structure of the brain, I strongly believe that, the natural process of matching the reason with a feeling, gives the uniqueness of what I call the *memorized information*.

The memorized information is in fact the piece of information that becomes personal information, particular and unique for each of the individuals, due to the *feeling* added to the generic information. When asking "why?", the answer you get might be just a generic response, based on logic and reasoning and there is no trace of feelings. On the other hand, when asking "how do you know?" what you do is recalling the feeling added to the generic information. By adding a feeling I mean, connecting the generic information to personal values, believes or experiences. Due to feelings added, the memorized information is kept in our brain forever.

Every piece of information we held in our mind is in there just because consciously or unconsciously we added feelings to that. This is why people are shocked when you ask: "how do you know?". You are forcing their brain to look on the memorized information warehouse and bring to life the *feeling* that made that common piece of information to become a particular piece of information.

The benefits of the memorized information are: the accuracy of the stored information, long term storage, easy when accessing and genuine when applying to present situations. Amazingly, feelings are genuine, authentic, the mask they wear is one. Due to these qualities, feelings give an immense power and meaning to a common or generic information.

You see, nothing happens in our brains without feelings, because feelings are everything! Feelings bring music to our life, they bring taste, images and smells too. Behind every of these sensory you can find memories, and memories are the result of the feelings added to the common or generic information. Every single piece of a memorized information is in our brain's warehouse, due to the *feeling* born when connecting the generic information to our inner world of values, believes and experiences. Every time we want to get that information outside we have to *remember and recall the feeling* added to it. Why is it important?

Imagine your mind like a warehouse where the pieces of memorized information are like bricks, they are laid in a way that makes the warehouse a labyrinth, strong and unique. Now, imagine you want to recall a certain piece of information. All you have to do is to ask yourself "why?" or look for "what?" question and the answer you get, says what is that piece of information you need. In order to start bringing outside that certain brick you are looking for, and be 100% sure that the brick that comes out is the right brick, you have to recall the feeling added to that piece of generic information you memorized sometimes in the past. The feeling is recalled by asking the" how do you know?"question. The process is a very simple one:

- Ask yourself "Why?" or "What?" question. Get the answer! Now, you know what piece of information you need!

- How do you know? Recall the feeling! Feel saturated with the answer of "how do you know?". This is how you find out, for sure, if the answer you got at step one is an authentic and accurate one. Be honest with yourself about what you feel! Accuracy comes with honesty

- Make the decision! Take the proper brick out and use it!

The brick in here is the metaphor for the piece of information we need at a certain point in our lives in order to take the best and smart decisions. In order to be sure the answer we get is the right answer, we recall the feeling that made that piece of information to be the memorized information. Let's go back to children, the perfect examples to understand how great human nature is by birth! When they are young enough, about 3-4 years old, they are still unshaped, unschooled and unshipped on patterns and customs, rules and expectations. Their brain is trained by birth to be simple, to get simplicity, and through simplicity to bring world in their lives, and they to match the world.

Education is supposed to bring simplicity at its most, to make people become smarter, to create genius as genius is about asking simple questions, giving simple answers so as to discover the yet unrevealed.

Can you imagine a hybrid between schooling and coaching?

When *schooling* creates fears or frustration, *coaching* to come and, by asking simple questions, to *enable* people to find their way to *success*.

Think about this! How would it be like for the education process to have coaching as an ongoing process that manages difficult situations and give people the invisible hand to climb up the tree to success?

While thinking about education and coaching working together, I was asking myself "how do you know that this is a smart decision to take? I don't have a specific reason or a determined project that based on some data could give some wise predictions, but I feel it is right. Feelings are everything, because they are the cocktail of the brain. For example, love is a feeling that has incommensurable ingredients that the brain is able to produce and this is why love is never explained like a rational process. How do I know that coaching and schooling could make a fantastic job together and people have success? I know because, only thinking about coaching and schooling together, thinking about my personal examples, I feel saturated with happiness!

I have so many examples of fears that children learn during schooling, and they don't know how to handle them and they become the adults that share and teach fears.

Think about the fear of being cheated by people, and therefore we teach our children how not to *trust* instead of how to handle *distrustful* situations and people, how to pass over, go further and build on somebody else's mistakes.

I do feel saturated with happiness when I think

about my children being coached to pass over this kind of fear, more powerful than the fear of water, flying or height.

How strong, confident, caring, smart and genuine my children would become if they would be coached to *trust* people, to know how to handle people that cheat them instead of being unhappy, suspicious, always having a keen eagle eye that trusts nothing!

"Look for saturation! Saturation is the word!" Dr. Bandler's voice sounded in my brain, in my heart and filled my body. I understood that the answer to the "how do you know ?"question, the secret of everything in life is saturation. Saturate your brain and your body with happiness and this is how you will find out the answer to "How do you know?"! When I say happiness or any other good, powerful feelings and saturation, I say living the feeling like being on God's highest cliffs.

Think about loving your children, and I think this is the strongest feeling among all feelings! If you ask someone "how do you know you love your children?" the answers varies a lot and might have some reasonable explanations such as "I give them money to study, pay the best vacation, spend time and have fun and so on" but pay attention to what you see than what you hear him/her saying! You'll see his eyes glittering with tears of love and affection, his face shining, his voice trembling and hands staying together. After a while, being tired of "how do you know?", he will say, "I know this and I can't explain myself using words!".

What you see in his eyes, when saying this, what you feel out from his voice, is called *saturation* and at that point, you get the proper authentic answer. Shiny faces and the happiest eyes ever seen, tell more than hundreds of reasons!

I took this is example to make myself clear to you what do I mean by saturation. I invite you to ask the "how do you know?" question every time you feel having a dilemma and you are not confident about the decision to take or already taken. Stop asking "how do you know?" only when you feel saturated with reasons, giving yourself reasonable explanations, or with feelings, the best and the strongest feelings ever felt before. This question is the question to success, it opens your brain and your heart, makes you see the unseen and hear the unheard.

Every time I coach people, during my coaching sessions, I meet amazing opportunities, and when I say opportunities, I refer to the lessons I learn when asking them questions. Asking questions make us brighter, more open minded and more susceptible when it comes about beliefs, rules and principles. You know what, I never feel surprised by the answers I get or the questions I receive, as I always expect human mind to be unpredictable, although the predictable side is difficult to be avoided, due to our leading nature(asking leading questions and giving leading answers).

 A few psychologists I met, said that people are always predictable, and they were so right, as they asked predictable questions. How can you expect to be asked an unpredictable question when your question is a targeted one?

If you don't challenge, the mind won't mind to deliver the expected or predicted answer to you, and here we are like in Pavlov's experiment turning on the light to get only saliva. I want to get more then saliva from my clients, or if I turn on the light, I want to see them doing things they were never thinking about: this is what I call brain exploration.

Brain exploration was my favorite subject when I coached one of my friends, an amazing painter. He was a great artist but not a good seller of his paintings. During our coaching sessions, one of the questions was:

"How many possibilities do you have to sell your paintings?" and the answer I got was:

"Well, I only have two possibilities: art galleries or some random expositions!"

Believe me, I wasn't surprised but amazed about the way his brain created very clear and specific limitations, the way his brain decided to have only two possibilities to sell the paintings! To me it was a sort of "Eureka!" and at that point I knew he was mine!

"Listen to this! How do you know that you have

only two possibilities?

"Well, as far as I know, an art gallery is probably the only place where the paintings are to be sold." he answered to me, pretty much convinced he was right. And he was right partially, because he never thought about his work like being a good that must bring money.

Rules and normality taught him that these are the only ways, and his brain decided to follow the rules, never question, never think outside of the box.

"Are your paintings about something, specifically, or about someone…even categories?"

 "Yes, they speak about some musicians!"

"Do you see these musicians having fans?"

 "Thousands of fans!" he replied to me

 "Where do you find them?"

"Oh, I can find them on socializing web sites, fun clubs" he replied with a big smile on his face, predicting the point I was going to touch.

"Now, listen! How many possibilities can you see when it comes about selling your paintings?"

"Oh, my God! Now, I know exactly what to do and there are so many ways! "

This was just the beginning, the beginning of a tremendous journey of his brain, and he was that smart to realize that by questions, and I mean smart and right questions, you can get anything. It is absolutely amazing how the brain is able to rethink, reorder priorities and actions only by asking the proper question! At that moment, the brain looks like a smart waterfall that finds a new way and floods it, as if it was a very well known, but deeply buried way. Looks like the brain woke up.

You can easily recognize this "brain waking up" by noticing the "Oh, yes!" expression on people' faces. So was my friend's mind, a waterfall! He got free and huge publicity, on web sites and TV shows, and publicity makes the difference when it comes about selling. He really expanded the area of opportunities, he increased his chances to sell his paintings, only when asking this simple, smart question:" how do you know?"

Do you know how it is like to look for a lifetime that question that makes the difference, gives you an answer, that answer that makes you cry in the loudest voice ever heard: "That's it!!!"? My friend knows this perfectly. He is still amazed about the way his life changed so quickly, discovering new opportunities and having huge chances to make the most of his life both as an artist and human being. Even more, he found out what coaching was by definition, using personal example. When I got this question from him:

"What is coaching?"

 I told him:

"Coaching is the best experience you'll have with yourself, and guess what? You are going to tell me later on what coaching is!"

I see coaching like a piece of art with a strange, but perfect architecture that enables us to change the bricks that live anywhere inside the building, without damaging the whole masterpiece. It is not a happening that coaching is about questions, it is amazing how people all over the world decided to return to simplicity by inventing this new science called Coaching.

Chapter 5

YES, WE CAN!

A challenge is not a valuable challenge if doesn't meet the right person. The right person is that person the challenge was born for. All I know is that everything is right on this planet, at a right time, on a right place, and we, all, call this sort of perfection, timing and matching, destiny. How many times in a lifetime we hear "it was meant to be!"? How many times we have on our lips the "why me?" question?

The 17of July 2003, an absolutely marvelous day of July to gave born to an amazing child, my son! God was playing with the mud of creation in His hands, making the most marvelous creature I ever seen, my son!

Two nights before I had a dream, that kind of dream I will never forget. I dreamed my unborn child and I could see his eyes, green, big eyes with a wide mouth and beautiful smile. He looked different! Different was the word that really crushed me, scared me, made me fill like being in the outer space. I couldn't breath anymore! I was feeling the power and the pressure of the word different. I woke up having tears in my eyes, he was moving inside me and I could feel his little hands.

"Are you ready, my love?" I asked him, matching his hands and for a second I had the feeling that my hand touched his hand. He was ready, ready for me and for his father, ready to challenge us and to make us be smarter, to care more, have faith, and never give up.

From the first day I held him in my arms, I knew that he was born for me and there was a reason I had him. You know, we all get what we can do, and there is no bigger stone than our capacity of carrying it on and on for a lifetime. And if you succeed in, guess what? The reward is another stone, a bigger one and this is because you proved you can.

I was watching my son growing up and I was wondering why my instinct says something is not right, although he was acting and doing things like a normal baby. Something in his eyes told me that I met features like his before…and I did.

7 years before, while going to a competition at Psychology I had as a subject "The methods and techniques used in teaching children with learning disabilities (children having High Functioning Autism and Williams Syndrome)".

Williams Syndrome kids were my favorite kids. I was in love with their capacity of loving and socializing, sometimes going to extreme, being excessively friendly. At that moment I was asked if I truly believe that I can manage a child with Williams Syndrome and my answer was that I can do it, no doubt about it!

7 years later, I took my son in to my arms and kept him so close to me that I could taste and smell the green of his eyes, a deep green like an

ocean and an intense green like an autumn grass! All I knew at that time was that together we can succeed in everything, that Williams Syndrome is just a challenge and there must be a top of a hill for these kids too, where they could perform at the highest standards and expectations!

What I know for sure about life, is that life is always about expectations! Until the moment I had my son, I never knew that there were two types of expectations:

- Negative expectations
- Positive expectations

The doctors that saw my son, gave me a list of negative expectations, telling me:

"Expect your son not to read and comprehend very well, not to add or multiply not to be able to remember the place he lives and come back home by himself and so on". Hearing all these things, I started seeing a huge black wall in front of my eyes and without verbalizing my brain asked me:

"What the hell he knows about my son? Who is he to predict my son's future just taking into account a list of Williams Syndrome disabilities? How dare he to give me that *not to do list?"*

Can you imagine that, all these kind of negative expectations are like subliminal messages that go to the brain of the parents, and the parents come back home like zombies repeating the *"not to do list"* to know it by heart and "teach" the child that *he can't, he is not able to...?*

Trust me, this is a bad plan, a very destructive one that opens the doors to the unlimited world of disabilities!

I wonder what the process is looking like when people choose between a bad plan and a good plan. What in our brain makes us consider first the bad plan instead of the good plan? I don't know what makes us choose one way or the other, but I know that our brain has a sort of attitude, and that attitude *can be trained.*

I see brain's attitude like the position decided to be taken by brain itself at a certain point, under certain circumstances and about a certain subject. It is a matter of taking decisions, so the brain has to decide either to feel good or to feel bad, favor or disfavor, like or dislike, be happy or unhappy. You know, if the brain decides to be happy, than he is going to have a good plan. If there is always a matter of choice, why not to train the brain to have always a good plan, be happy for instance?

But what is a good choice? The general definition, in my opinion, would be that the good choice is that choice that brings success and happiness together in an interdependency relationship. The only problem I see in practice is that, people are wrongly asked if they want to have a good plan, instead of asking them:

"You want to have success and be happy, don't you? *"First,* d*irect them to the feeling created by having a good plan, not ask them about the process of choosing a good plan. Saturate your brain first with feeling of success and happiness, then direct your brain into action by having a good plan.*

It is like you tell to your brain:

"See, this is how success and happiness taste like, if you want more let's talk about it!"

Success and happiness are the two amazing things that my son wants. I never ask him if he wants to have a good plan regarding a challenge, I ask him:

"You want to be the best, have fun and be happy, don't you?

His immediate response is verbal and nonverbal, the same: "YES!"

This being the first step, I go to the second step and ask him *what he thinks he has to do* in order to be happy, so I direct his brain to planning and he, without knowing consciously, he is having a good plan.

So, first, taste the feeling and then draw the process of a good plan! Surprisingly, this is how the brain works! Change brain chemistry first, because later on, the chemistry works for you, doing amazing things!

The more he succeeds in, the more he is willing to go to the next step and he is embracing any challenge he meets like an opportunity. My son found Mathematics unpleasant and very difficult, while the Romanian and English languages very funny, interesting and easy to deal with. The real challenge I met while working with my son, was to change his brain chemistry, the way his brain felt about Mathematics. Mathematics was an issue for my son because his brain decided that, his brain decided to have a bad plan regarding this subject. So as to create a new good feeling about an issue, you can choose either to give born to a totally new feeling, by coaching that person, or you can take an existing good feeling, related to another similar issue and simply paste it. What I chose to do, as it always works better like this for children, was to take the feeling created by his success at Romanian and English languages and pasted it on Mathematics. So, the next step taken was to identify the amazing feeling that was going to be pasted on. Before copying and pasting, that feeling must be decrypted and this is made by relating and connecting the feeling to one of the sensory modalities that applies the most to that person. When it comes about sensory modalities, my son is gustatory/olfactory and auditory. He was telling me that, for instance, a good mark at Romanian language tasted like something very sweet and sounded like a violin playing. That was the best decrypted feeling I needed to paste it on Mathematics. I took these storied descriptions and I asked him what he thinks about hearing the violin playing every single time he was going to deal with Mathematics? He was so delighted that I could see an amazing sparkling light in his eyes! At that moment, I knew his brain was hungry for success and happiness!

He was concerned about how could we succeed in, because Mathematics was for sure not as easy as his mother language. So, being concerned and not fully saturated with success and happiness, he passed quickly to the process, worrying about the process and actions to be taken *The key is to let the child go naturally to the process only if he is not worried but saturated with eagerness, let's do-it attitude and trust.*

If you see worries never go to the process, but go back to the feeling created by success and make sure he gets saturated with this feeling.

I saw my son being concerned and worried, so I went for persuasion, making sure that he wanted success no matter how difficult Mathematics was. I used the same persuasion process as in sales when people came up with any kind of objections and fears. What I am saying here is not that my son turned into a genius or he is an Olympic at Mathematics. He is succeeding at so many tests, he is having the courage to go for any challenge and take every opportunity he encounters, not worrying, but constantly canalizing his energy and abilities in order to get success.

People will always buy success and happiness and they will always want around them people that have and share success and happiness. Now, we know that, first, after saturating our brain and body with the feeling created by success, we can train our brain to have a good attitude regarding a challenge and choose to always have a good plan.

The question is: how can we do this? *Conserve and Convert!* This is what I found out when working with my son and other people as well.

Conservation always goes to the good habits and good behavioral patterns. On these abilities we can rely our process and we can go further and build the positive attitude so as to have the best outcome. These abilities, positive attitudes, good behavioral patterns are in fact our strong points. This list containing the strong points, lives there inside us, and it can be extended every time we have good plans and make good choices. This is how we create new positive attitudes and good behaviors like being in a spiral game that never ends. Fortunately, when practicing conservation, we always discover new abilities, capacities and by using them into practice, living them daily, they become behaviors.

The magic of the conserving process is that, every time we meet a challenge, we unconsciously and naturally recall our positive attitudes and good behaviors. While practicing the recalled positive attitudes and good behaviors, we are going to discover new abilities and capacities that naturally live inside our brain. Then, every time we go for conserving and we recall the ability discovered before and practice it, over time, this ability turns into a behavior. The conclusion is that, practicing conserving is a way of discovering new abilities and creating new behaviors.

Behaviors are like bridges: complex to build, hard

to maintain during time and difficult to replace when situations require. When it comes to good behaviors, the challenge is to maintain them and here comes the Conservation process. When it comes about bad and destructive behaviors, the challenge is to replace or reeducate them so here we talk about *Conversion*. I, deliberately, decided to go for conversion of the bad behaviors and not for *extermination,* mainly because sometimes, these behaviors could be useful to us at a certain point.

There is nothing inside us born or build without any specific purpose or reason. We are like a huge airport with billions of planes that will always have a reason to fly and a final destination to reach at. When reaching to the final destination, nothing is lost or forgotten, everything is being conserved and when the time and the situation require, a new trip is planned for that behavior and a new adventure rises up inside us.

Conservation and Conversion is the simplest process that I always apply to people I work with, and the most common example that comes into my mind is that, when people talk to each other and they get tensed, anxious or nervous, they are really able to *replace* this bad behavior that disturbs their listening process and influence in a negative way the outcome. Imagine that, they are able to *relocate* the bad behavior and the bad energy somewhere else: for example, in a pen they held in the hand, or in an imaginary box that they can visualize it and they can move it, lock it or thrown it away, as they decide.

All they had to do was to have this concept in their minds and make it happen in practice by *stopping the first bad reaction and go for response. While coming up with the response, conversion goes to the bad behavior and turns this one into something positive and constructive.* The outcome is an amazing mixture between a conserved behavior and a converted one. This outcome brings self awareness, success, creates network and opens the inner doors to new opportunities, challenges and possibilities

Conserve and convert-something that I did not invent as actions for sure, but as a process, truly. It is indeed in our nature to act conservation and conversion, but it is not quite in our nature to make the two of them work together.

Together they form a concept, an easy one, easy to remember and most important, easy to move us to action and make the difference. Positive attitude makes the difference!

What we should always remember is that during *reaction or response* processes, the brain brings the best of us or the worst of us, as *we choose*. Mainly, when it comes about reacting, conversion process barely goes, hardly exists. Reaction as an impulse, comes all of a sudden, so there is a less possibility of bringing conserving and conversion together and have a deliberative process, so, the stronger of the two sets of behaviors wins: either a good behavior or a bad behavior and therefore we will have a good reaction or a bad reaction.

When reacting, we don't choose, as reaction is an impulse. If we react in a good way, or in bad way, the outcome is a good one or a bad one. So, it is a matter of taking the risk.

When responding, we choose, because our *brain has the possibility and time to think*. And thinking is a really a smart thing, isn't it? There is no risk while responding, because the brain takes the time to think, the brain decides to have a good plan so as to get the best outcome ever. The brain really sees the benefits and weights them. What *conserving and converting do?* They force us to think!

I really enjoyed working with people, and in some particular situations I saw them unable to convert anger into something constructive while reacting to an event or a challenge. The same people that had in their minds the *conserve and convert* concept, were able to convert anger into motivation, a sort of "let's do it" attitude when responding to the same event.

My piece of advice is: Never react! Always go for responding because responding involves thinking and thinking means connecting, putting pieces together to work like a wise clock!

Instinctively, people run away from other people that have a bad or destructive reaction instead of a proper response(by proper response I mean the response that creates an outcome that brings benefits to both of the parties involved in) to an event that challenged them and took them out of their comfort zone. We don't like reactions, bad reactions and still we find difficult not to react when an event occurs and moves us out of our zone where we feel so comfortable. I can say that brain knows brains, and exactly like a single drop of water that moves the ocean and the circles created are the measure of its sensitivity to similarity, in the same way, one brain is sensitive to similarity and detects other brains, predicting behaviors. Usually, brain sensitivity to similarity go to predictability and predictability means fore thinking.

There is no need for friendship background so as two stranger brains to have expectations from each other, to wait for a response not for a bad reaction, to predict behaviors based on being sensitive to similarity. If a brain expects another brain to have attitude don't you think it's simple to expect for self attitude? It is simple indeed, but when it comes about putting into practice the brain's chemistry, simplicity is quite a challenge.

Every time I meet a disabled person, the feeling

of being blessed and challenged surrounds me, making me being open and sympathetic. Can you imagine that a great majority of people have more negative expectations than positive expectations regarding disability and they never feel blessed or challenged when meeting this kind of people? I am positive that my attitude regarding disabled people will never treat disability because a genetic disorder stays a genetic disorder, but if normality is relative, why shouldn't success be relative? Why to give up on expectations just because what we name success is so absolute, that there is no place for successful stories, for real winners that really surpasses their condition?

What I have learned from practice, while working with people is that, no matter if we talk about persuading people around us or self persuasion, creating expectations for other people or creating self expectations, always it's about brain attitude. There is something extremely valuable that makes the difference and brings success, making even a disabled learning child be on the top of a hill, achieve goals, grow and develop. That valuable something that change "a story " into" the story", a disabled person into a different able person, is the powerful imperative *"yes, you can!"*

This is the perfect imperative that is spreading power everywhere, injects trust and confidence, highlights his or her strong points, opening the door to the vast world of opportunities.

It is time for persuasion! It is time for shocking the brain, as disability means "not being able" and we need to wake up the brain with the "Yes, you can!" There are no disabled children but different able children, so all we have to do is to adjust the methods and techniques and change the way we approach disability.

This first step is the one where we can build self-starter attitude and we need to focus on building and increasing self confidence.

Self confidence looks like a strong tree that must have deep and strong roots in order to face any wind blowing First step is to plant that tree, gain their trust to let you inside their mind and heart. Trust is gained only by being genuine, authentic when influencing and persuading. Then you have to bring your power and transfer to them, making them wishing to create self expectations.

Let them imagine, visualize success! Encourage them to see and feel each single step they take, as mission accomplished, goal achieved and key to both success and happiness! Feed them with their success and spread the feeling in their body! This is the way we put water at the roots of the self confidence tree. The stronger and influential self confidence becomes, more freedom and power that person gains. Freedom is the pure expression of responsibility, capacity of assuming both ways: success and failure too.

You see, self confidence it is about facing success as well as failure, without being disappointed, or bringing in the excuse of "being disabled".

In the moment they start trusting themselves and meeting their expectations, they are ready to face the world and its expectations. There is no fear, there are no worries, no bad plans but eagerness to learn the new lessons that opportunities bring to them. The level of the self confidence can be measured in so many ways, but the best indicator saying that self confidence is a really strong tree, is when these people never complain about their state, they never use their genetic disorder as an excuse for failure, for inactivity, for not dreaming, daring and expecting.

Naturally, when my son has to perform new difficult tasks, he starts worrying and that is the perfect moment when I have to interfere and persuade him that there is no place for disability and I inject confidence. The key to success is to listen to them carefully, to really pay attention to the words they say and treat their fear by injecting confidence, calming them down and assure them that both, success and failure are valuable ways to progress, grow and development.

I treasure my children the way they are. As far as I am concerned, I am not going to turn a daffodil into a rose while growing it up, just because the rest of the world prefers a rose than a daffodil. A good gardener does the best for the flowers he grows in his garden without conditioning them, caring for them differently only because some of them are more expensive on a market

My mission as a mother is to ensure my children' environment, to create space and time for their development, to trust them and make them trust themselves and people around them. Their self confidence is looking like a strong medicine, that immunize their mind, making them be able to grow up and influence, to share love and forgive, to be wise and let things go when time comes.

Now, my son knows that he can, that a genetic disorder is just a condition not a destiny and he taught me the wisest lesson of my life: "Relativity belongs more to human beings than to Physics"

Chapter 6

LOVE AND PERSUASION

Love, as Adam and Eve, is the right beginning for everything, the fundamental condition for all the things that come with love or after love, to exist, to produce change and create adaptation.

Wouldn't be great to have a chemical formula for love and inject it in the brain? Imagine how many great things people could achieve if they knew what chemical formula to put in the brain cocktail in order to produce love! I saw many people that were asked to follow the plan they chose to go with, to practice discipline constantly if they want to accomplish the goals and have success. They followed the plan for a while, and then they failed because there was no foundation such as love and passion.

How can you practice discipline when you are not even in there? It is impossible to be disciplined if you don't love what you do, if you are not 100% committed and committing comes with love. It is said that the discipline is the bridge between goals and accomplishments, but what makes the bridge to be sustainable is the engineering of love and persuasion.

We could go far back away in time and going from novels and romance to engineering and science, love and persuasion made the team and they were together like in the chain of a mutual feeding and growing.

Think about Jane Austen's novel "Persuasion", that speaks about the magic of love, the love that brings magic, gives wings to fly, love that hurts and deceives, but no matter what, love is always able to persuade! In order to persuade and to be persuaded, you have to have deep down the roots of love. I feel that Einstein was able to go so far and be so persuasive due to his love for Physics. His genius was a perfect mixture between native intelligence, knowledge, genuine love and passion

Genius is not about genetics only, it is not a state or a disorder, genius brings the chemistry of love of its most. Geniuses are born with the chemical formula for love at a level that they never need to be fed again. This is how success comes to them, and they succeed in influencing, in being highly persuasive! Their brain is saturated with love and passion for what they do!

And in the name of love, sometimes, you may hurt others, you may get hurt and at that point, love needs to be persuaded. It happened once that I saw a cat carrying its kittens to the shelter. It was raining outside, and the cat took each of its kittens, grabbing their necks. While doing this, it happened that one of them got hurt...I could see blood on the cat's teeth. My daughter, who was there with me watching the entire scene, became angry and confused all of a sudden:

Sarah: "Look mum, can you see the blood on the mother's teeth? What kind of mother is this cat? When you start hurting your child, there is no longer love!"

Laura: "Do you think so?" I asked her looking

into her eyes, copying her body posture and rising up the right eyebrow (as she did)

Laura: "Tell me, my dear! Why do you think, the cat is caring its kitten to the shelter?"

Sarah: "The cat wants to protect its kitten from the rain!"

Laura: "That's right! What's the reason the cat is doing this?"

Sarah: "The cat is doing this because they are its children!"

Laura: "She is doing this from love, right?"

Sarah: "Yes, but love had hurt the kitten!"

Laura: "Yes, you are right, my sweet heart! That kitten might hurt now, but, you know what? It is safe… and later on, there is going to be no blood, no wound, no pain! I do the same when I ask you to stop your computer gaming. At that point, you are angry, you cry and you might think that I am not doing that from love.

Laura:" Caring about your eyes, don't you think is

coming from love?" Caring about your education and security, isn't it an act of love?"

You see, I and the cat might come from different worlds, but when it comes to love, genuine love, we are not different, not at all! We have children, and children are the measure of supreme love, as well as the result of supreme love."

That was an amazing example that nature gave to us, the nature helped me persuade my love for my daughter when I was searching for a way to prove my love for her. To become smarter and smarter every day, to need no particular formulas created in order to persuade, we have to pay attention to the nature, to listen to it and return to simplicity. Wisdom has no curvy ways and wisdom is always like a simple coat that fits to summer as well to winter.

Persuasion lives inside us and the more love we bring in, the more genuine, authentic persuasion we experience.

Lack of the persuasion ability is in fact lack of authenticity, lack of genuinely as persuasion is not a script that can be learnt by heart and practiced like a cold rational procedure. Persuasion is the magic cocktail of the brain that comes out from the heart and speaks powerfully on everybody's tongue.

Persuasion is influencing; either we appeal logic and reason, or feelings and emotions, but no one can influence somebody else's beliefs, attitude, or behaviors if the process of influencing is not a process streamed from love and passion.

Imagine that the most well known techniques of persuasion such as reciprocity, commitment and consistency, social proof, and liking are based on love and passion. Love gives power to persuasion, and if we want to come back to Nelson Mandela or Martin Luther King, we see that the immense power of influencing came from their unique way of living their values, of valuing knowledge and art of speaking to people, no matter the language, despite religion and color differences. For them, love was at its most, and yes, they were genius of love so therefore genius of influencing.

The most valuable thing to remember is that; no

matter if you talk about buying, selling, marketing and advertising or even more so, about parenting, you will always go for persuasion and influencing. And if you look for wealth and survival you must be genuine while influencing, you must persuade with passion and love. What is more interesting is that while doing this, you don't have to wonder and worry about the way the brain of the people you influence is working.

You don't have to look for scripts and speeches to sell the proper idea or feeling to the left or to the right hemisphere of the brain, to the left or to the right prefrontal cortex of the brain, you will speak powerfully, genuinely…*you will influence*!

Influencing is winning over people; it is not about defeating them! Influencing is the grace of the *power* and the beauty of the *love* that live in the genuine human nature.

CONCEPTS and TOOLS USED IN THIS BOOK

1. *The Pyramid of Persuasion*

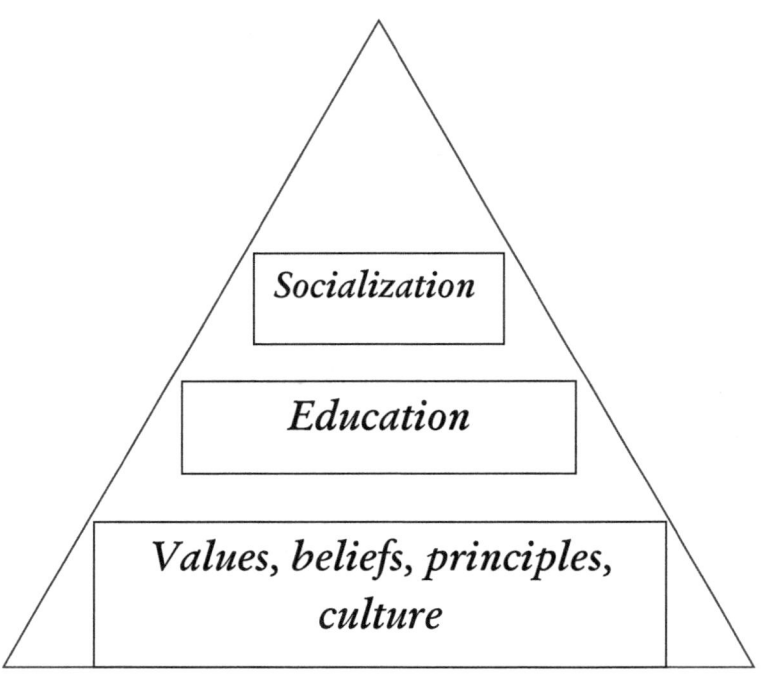

Values, beliefs and principles are at the base of the pyramid meaning that if we persuade from here we'll be genuine, credible and powerful, 100% of persuasion process coming from here, has 100% chances for success. Your own values say "who you are", "where do you want to go", "how do you work".

The second level of pyramid talks about *education* and I call this level, the level where you have the chance to specialize and differentiate your persuasion process by treating client's fears and objections. Persuasion must come from the base (values, beliefs and culture) and then take some more power from the second level.

The third level of the pyramid is the *socialization* and this is mostly about that ability of working with others. Being on the top, socialization is like the chocolate you put on a vanilla ice cream, it makes the difference.

The magic of this pyramid consists in going from down to top and never going from top to down or miss one of the three levels.

If you want to be the master of influencing, and make persuasion bring success to you, live and practice this pyramid!

2. *The Spiral of Existence*

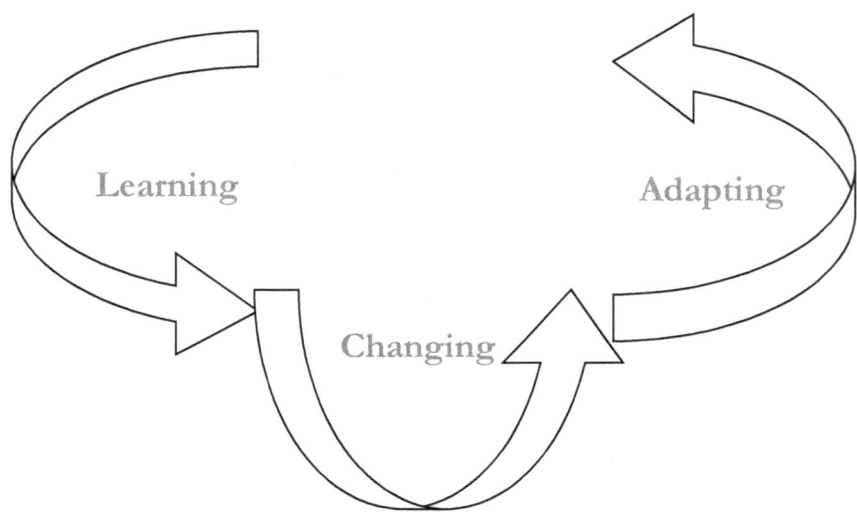

This spiral talks about the way these three major notions: Learning, Changing and Adapting work together and influence our existence.

- Learning – it is the process of assimilating information.
- Changing is a consequence of the learning process, showing that the information we accessed was able to produce something

inside us. This is a way of measuring the success of the learning process

- Adapting is about everything, it is the end of the changing process and the beginning for new learning processes. It is not enough to make changes and to acknowledge them, you have to do more in order to be successful, and this is to adapt.

The key to success is to live and practice this spiral and to make sure that the *adapting* process is really ended and meantime ready to create a new opportunity for a new learning process.

While adapting, a new *brain path is created and a new behavior pattern is going to be seen* when interacting or meeting the stimuli. The stronger this new brain path becomes, the weaker the old brain path that was destructive becomes. In order to see if the adapting process was completed, you have to make sure the former stimuli that was linked to the destructive behavior, has no impact on the new brain path (the new path created in the brain doesn't recognize that old stimuli).

2. *The memorized information*

The memorized information is in fact that piece of generic information that became personal information, particular and unique for each of individuals due to he *feelings* added to it.

Every piece of information we held in our mind is in there because consciously or unconsciously, we added feelings to it.

This is why people are shocked when you ask: "how do you know?". You are forcing their brain to look on the memorized information warehouse and bring to life the *feeling* that made that common piece of information to become a particular piece of information.

The benefits of the memorized information are: the accuracy of the stored information, long term storage, easy when accessing and genuine when applying to present situations. Amazingly, feelings are genuine, authentic, the mask they wear is one. Due to these qualities, feelings give an immense power and meaning to a common or generic information. Always trust the feeling!

3. *Conserve and Convert*

This concept makes the difference between reacting and responding to an event that takes us out of our comfort zone.

Conservation always goes to the good habits, good behavioral patterns and on these abilities we can rely our process, we can go further and build the positive attitude so as to have the best outcome.

Behaviors are like bridges: complex to build, hard to maintain during time and difficult to replace when situations require. When it comes to good behaviors, the challenge is to maintain them and here comes the Conservation process. When it comes about bad and destructive behaviors, the challenge is to replace or reeducate them so here we talk about *Conversion*. I, deliberately, decided to go for conversion of the bad behaviors and not for *extermination*, mainly because sometimes, these behaviors could be useful to us at a certain point. When facing an event that takes us out of our comfort zone, all we have to do is to have this concept in our minds and make it happen in practice by stopping first bad reaction and go for response. When choosing to go for responding, conversion goes to the bad behavior and turns this one into something positive and constructive. In some cases, minimizing the bad behavior, for example until it is looking like a small white spot that you can put it into your pocket, might be a very smart option.

Remember!

When reacting, we don't choose, reaction is like an impulse and if we react in a good way, or in bad way, the outcome is a good one or a bad one. So, it is a matter of taking the risk.

When responding, we choose, because our *brain has the possibility and time to think*. And thinking is a really a smart thing, isn't it? There is no risk while responding, because the brain takes the time to think, the brain decides to have a good plan so as to get the best outcome ever. The brain really sees the benefits and weights them. What *conserving and converting do?* They force us to think!

I really enjoyed working with people, and in some particular situations I saw them unable to convert anger into something constructive while reacting to an event or a challenge. The same people that had in their minds the *conserve and convert* concept, were able to convert anger into motivation, a sort of "let's do it" attitude when responding to the same event.

My piece of advice is: Never react! Always go for responding because responding involves thinking and thinking means connecting, putting pieces together to work like a wise clock!

ABOUT THE AUTHOR

Laura Ion started her own business in coaching and training, after more than 15 years of professional experience in management and leadership, sales and training. She is recognized for charisma, motivation and influence, her speeches being admired and regarded as lessons to be followed.

Having background in Economy and Psychology, an authentic nature for persuasion and leading, she gained people' confidence and admiration.

She is a Licensed Practitioner of NLP and Licensed Practitioner of NHR of The Society of Neuro-Linguistic Programming, being trained by Dr. Bandler and his team.

Most importantly, Laura is the happiest mother of a child having Williams Syndrome and she is guiding him, joining him in his journey to a magnificent world of new challenges, possibilities and opportunities.

Laura's son's success is her success; therefore she speaks powerfully from her experience, from her value of love represented by her family.

If you want to enhance your life, make the most of your nature, gain happiness and success, read this book and the other that will come.

www.ingramcontent.com/pod-product-compliance
Lightning Source LLC
Chambersburg PA
CBHW070200290526
45789CB00002B/847